L A D I E S

23 ARRANGEMENTS FOR LADIES' CHOIR OR ENSEMBLE

BY TOM FETTKE

Lillenas Publishing Co.
KANSAS CITY, MO 64141

CONTENTS

Forever

CLAIRE CLONINGER

JOHN ROSASCO
Arr. by Doug Holck
SSA arr. by Tom Fettke

NOTE: an individual cassette accompaniment tape is available for this arrangement (MU-1201C).

15
dreams, come and go.
all, what are they?
stand, soon we're gone.
stand, soon we're gone.
15
21
But He is the peace in our lives
But He is the joy that en - dures;
But He is the love that re - mains;
Ah that re -
21
That sur - vives, for we know:
We are sure He will stay.
Tho' we change, He goes on.
mains; we change, He goes on.

28
slightly accented
All
He is for - ev - er and ev - er, And nev - er will
He is for - ev - er and ev - er, For time can't de -
He is for - ev - er and ev - er, Our Fa - ther a -
33
cease. He is the Lord of peace.
stroy. He is the song of joy.
bove. He is the heart of love.
37
He is for - ev - er and ev - er, And nev - er will
He is for - ev - er and ev - er, And time can't de -
He is for - ev - er and ev - er, Our Fa - ther a -
42
Unison
mf
3rd time to Coda
cease; Our nev - er end - ing, ev - er -
stroy;
bove;
mf

1

last - ing peace.

51

2

joy. Praise the

61

f

Lord, He will nev - er cease.

f

66

Praise the Lord, He is joy and

69 72

peace.

D.S. al Coda

CODA

80

last - ing, nev - er

84
end - ing love.
87
1st Sop. and Alto Praise the
f
Lord, for He reigns a -
2nd Sop: Praise the Lord, for He reigns a -
bove.
92
Praise the Lord, for the
bove.
Praise the Lord, for the
95
Lord is love.
Praise the
Lord is love.
Praise the

98
Lord, for He reigns a - bove.
Lord, for He reigns a - bove.
Praise the
103
Lord, for the Lord is
Praise the Lord, for the Lord is
106
cued 4th part opt.
ff
love,
is
ff
111
love.
8va

A Perfect Heart

R. R. and D. M.

REBA RAMBO and DONY McGUIRE
Arr. by Tom Fettke

C/E Dm C B♭/C C

tal - ents, Stand in awe of One so great; Now my

F add9 F A B♭add9 B♭ F/A Gm/B♭ F/C

slight accel.

soul be - gins to sing out To the Source

slight accel.

C13 C7 F

f

from which it came. Bless the

21 C ♩ = ca. 66 Dm7 C/E C7/E

strict rhythm

Lord who reigns in

f

strict rhythm

B♭/F F C Dm7 C/E C7/E B♭/F F C F

beau - ty; Bless the Lord who reigns with wis-dom and with pow'r. Bless the

25
C Dm7 C/E Smoothly C7/E
mf A7/E A7/5♯ A7 Dm B♭m/D♭ F/C F
Lord who fills my life with so much love, He can make
Smoothly
mf
B♭/C C B♭/F F B♭6/F F
a per - fect heart.
Bless the
f
Div.
29
C Dm7 C/E C7/E
Lord who reigns in
Bless the Lord who reigns in
f
B♭/F F
beau - ty;
Bless the
C Dm7 C/E
Lord who reigns with
B♭/F F C F
wis - dom and with pow'r.
beau - ty;
Bless the Lord who reigns with wis - dom and with pow'r.
Bless the
33
C Dm7 C/E C7/E A7/E A7/5♯ A7 Dm B♭m/D♭
Lord who fills my life with so much love, He can
Bless the Lord who fills my life with so much love, He can
Smoothly
mf

*A cappella preferred - accompaniment optional.

46

Lord ___ who reigns in beau - ty; Bless the Lord ___ who reigns with

wis - dom and _ with pow'r. _ Bless the

50

Lord ___ who fills my life with so much

love, He can make a per - fect

gradual decresc.

heart, A per - fect

gradual decresc.

54

heart, a per - fect heart,

pp

a per - fect heart.

pp

Proclaim the Glory of the Lord

D. L. and N. B.

DWIGHT LILES and NILES BOROP
Arr. by Doug Holck
SSA arr. by Tom Fettke

mf
15
fess He reigns; Lift up His name in prais - es for - ev - er. Pro - claim the
glo - ry of the Lord, make known His might-y deeds to all; Take up the call, let
Div. f
20
ev - 'ry na - tion know. He is our Mes - si - ah, our
f
Sav - ior and our King. Let all our voic - es join as one and fill the earth with sing - ing.

24
subito mp
Glo - ry to our God, His great - ness we ap - plaud; Let ev - 'ry
subito mp
f
race on ev - 'ry shore Pro - claim the glo - ry
28
2nd time to Coda
1st and 2nd Sop.
of the Lord.
the glo - ry of the Lord.
Alto
the glo - ry of the Lord.
31
mp

34
mf
Pro - claim the glo - ry of the
mf
Pro - claim the glo - ry of the
34
mf
Lord, give hon - or to the Prince of Peace; For if we cease the stones will start
Lord, give hon - or to the Prince of Peace; For if we cease the stones will start
38
shout - ing. Pro - claim the glo - ry of the Lord with hands up - lift - ed;
shout - ing. Pro - claim the glo - ry of the Lord with hands up - lift - ed;
38

D.S. al Coda
Div. f
Let us raise im - mor - tal praise to Him who reigns on high. He is
f
Let us raise im - mor - tal praise to Him who reigns on high. He is
D.S. al Coda
f
CODA
mf
of the Lord, the glo - ry of the Lord. He is
mf
46
f
our Mes - si - ah, our Sav - ior, and our King. Let all our voic - es join as one and
f

50
fill the earth with sing - ing. Glo - ry to our God, His great-ness we ap-plaud; Let
54
cresc.
ev - 'ry race on ev - 'ry shore Pro - claim the glo - ry, pro-claim the
cresc.
58
of the
glo-ry, Pro-claim the glo-ry, pro - claim the glo - ry, pro-claim the glo-ry of the
ff
Lord!
ff

He Giveth More Grace

ANNIE JOHNSON FLINT

HUBERT MITCHELL
Arr. by Doug Holck
SSA arr. by Tom Fettke

Warmly ♩ = ca. 96
mp
l.h.
5
Ped
Unison
mp
9
He giv - eth more grace when the bur - dens grow
13
great - er; He send - eth more strength when the la - bors in - crease. To

NOTE: an individual cassette accompaniment tape is available for this arrangement (MU-1220C).

Div.
21
added affliction He addeth His mercy; To multiplied
Unison
mf
25
trials, His multiplied peace. His love has no
mf
29
Div.
limit; His grace has no measure; His pow'r has no
slight rit.
33
a tempo
boundary known unto men. For out of His
slight rit.
a tempo

slightly slower
Unison mf
f
in - fi - nite rich - es in Je - sus, He
3
slightly slower
38
mp
giv - eth, and giv - eth, and giv - eth a - gain. When
mp
42
Tempo I
we have ex - haust - ed our store of en - dur - ance, When
46
our strength has failed ere the day is half done, When

50
More rhythmic and building
Div.
we reach the end of our hoard - ed re - sourc - es, Our
54
Fa - ther's full giv - ing is on - ly be - gun.
mf
58
Building with intensity and excitement
Div.
For His love has no lim - it; His grace has no mea - sure; His
mf
62
f
rit.
mf
66
a tempo, building
pow'r has no bound - a - ry known un - to men. For out of His
f
rit.
mf
a tempo, building

rit.
ff
mp
in - fi-nite rich - es in Je - sus,
He
rit.
ff
72
1st and 2nd Sop.
rit.
Rubato
75
a tempo
and giv - eth a - gain and a -
giv - eth, He giv - eth and giv - eth a - gain, a
Alto
giv - eth, He giv - eth
72
75
mp
rit.
Rubato
a tempo
gain, a - gain,
rit.
a - gain.
gain and a - gain and a - gain, a - gain.
a - gain and a - gain.
rit.

Victory in Jesus
E. M. B.
EUGENE M. BARTLETT
Arr. by Tom Fettke
With great energy
Broadly
Tempo I ♩ = ca. 116
1. I heard an old, old story, how a Savior came from glory, How He gave His life on Calvary to save a wretch like me. I heard about His groaning, of His precious blood's a-
(3. I) heard about a mansion He has built for me in glory, And I heard about the streets of gold beyond the crystal sea, About the angels singing, and the old redemption

18
C/G G Em Cm6/E♭ G/D B7/D♯ Em Em7 Am7 C/D D7
ton - ing. Then I re - pent - ed of my sins and won the vic - to -
sto - ry; And some sweet day I'll sing up there the song of vic - to -
22
G Stronger C/G G G7 C C/E
ry. O vic - to - ry in Je - sus, my Sav - ior, for -
ry.
Heavier
26
C/G G Em Cm6/E♭ G/D G A9 A7add6 A9
ev - er! He sought me and bought me with His re - deem - ing
30
D D13/7 G C/G G
blood. He loved me ere I knew Him, and
3
3

34
2nd time to Coda
C C/G G Bm/F♯ Em
all my love is due Him. He plunged me to
Bm Em7 Am9 Am7 C/D D7 G
rit.
vic - to - ry ___ be - neath the cleans - ing flood.
Solo (or unison)
F/G Slowly, with warmth
mp
2. I
rit.
mp
39
Cadd9 C B♭/C C7 F6 F F/C C
heard a - bout His heal - ing, of His cleans-ing pow'r re - veal - ing, How He
43
Am Am7♯ Am7 C6/D D7sus D7 G7sus G7
made the lame to walk a - gain and caused the blind to see. And

47 Cadd9 C Gm7 C7 F6/C F/C F/C C G/B

then I cried, "Dear Je - sus, come and heal my bro - ken spir - it"; And

51 Am Fm/A♭ Fm6/A♭ C/G G♯o Am Dm7 F/G G7 C

gradual accel. to tempo I

some - how Je - sus came and brought to me the vic - to - ry.

gradual accel. to tempo I

C/D D.S. al Coda CODA Bm E7

All ff

3. I vic - to - ry be -

mf ff

8ve

59 Am7 C/D G fff

neath the cleans - ing flood. Vic - to - ry!

fff

8ve 8ve

He Loved Me

D. H.

DOUG HOLCK and TOM FETTKE

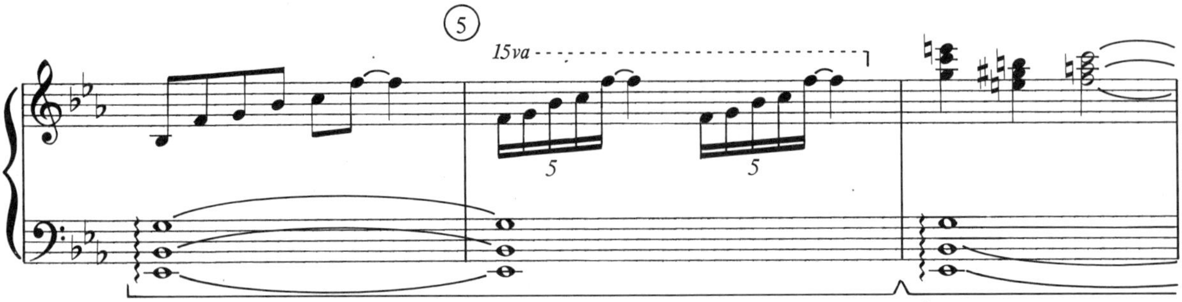

Ethereal ♩ = ca. 60

pp

R.H.

15va

(5)

15va

F add⁹

p

Cm⁷/F   B♭/F   B♭m/F

Narration: God chose us to be His very own before the creation of the world. "He decided then to make us

D♭/E♭   A♭/E♭   E♭sus   E♭

(13) holy in his eyes, without a single fault—we who stand before him covered with his love. His unchanging plan has always been to adopt us into his own family by sending Jesus Christ to die for us. And he did this because he wanted to!" (Eph. 1:4-5, TLB) .

NOTE: an individual cassette accompaniment tape is available for this arrangement (MU-2030C).

17
Deliberately but sustained
Eb
mp
Solo or unison
Abm/Eb
Eb
He chose me
be-fore the world was known. He chose me
mp
Abm/Eb
21
Gm
Gm7 5b/C
C7 9b
to be His ver - y own.
He made me,
then let me choose my
Fm
Ab/Bb
Bb7
25
Eb
way.
I chose to
move a - way.
He loved me
Abm/Eb
Eb
Abm/Eb
when hope had tak-en wing. He
loved me
when I lost ev - 'ry-thing.

29

Gm7 — Gm7 5♭/C — C9♭ 7 — Fm

slight accel.

He bought — me; re-demp-tion's work was done — through Je-sus

slight accel.

Ab/Bb — a tempo — Ab — G7 9♯ 5♯ — rit. — G7 9♭ 5♯

34 More movement

Cmadd9 — Cm

mf *All unison*

Christ, His Son. Who — shall sep - a -

8va 8va

a tempo — rit. — 8va 8va

mf More movement

Cm/Bb — F/A — Fm/Ab — G7sus — G7

sub. mp

rate me from the love of — God? Shall

mp

38

C — Fm6/C — *mf* — Cm

dreams of to - mor - row, pain, or —

42
Slightly stronger
Fm6/C
Eb/Bb
AbM7/Bb
Ab6/Bb
Bb7
sor - row? Can the need of food or earth - ly pos - ses - sions, The
8va
threat of war or man's op - pres - sion?
46
Emphatically
mf
Div.
In all these
things
cresc.
vic - t'ry is our re - ward;
Eb
Eb/Db
Db
Abadd9/C
Ab/C
50
F7/C
Cm
Bbm add9
Bbm
Gb
Fm
Ebm7
decresc.
Vic - t'ry is our re - ward through Je - sus

Christ, our Lord.
rit.
8va
mp
55
Warmly
Unison
mp
Of this I am
a tempo
sure, that nei-ther death, nor life, nor an - gels, nor prin-ci -
a tempo, smoothly
pal - i - ties, Nor pow - ers, nor things pres - ent, nor things to
60
Div.
mf
mf
come, Not height, nor
64
Broad, majestic and with great confidence
ff
f
ff

Eb/Db
Ab/C
Gb/Bb
decresc.
depth, nor any creature Shall separate me from the
decresc.
68
Gb/Ab
Ab7
Ebm
Db/F
Ebm/Gb
Go
Ebm7/Ab
mf
Unison
slight rit.
71
Dbadd9
Db
love of God. Of this I am sure, that neither
mf
slight rit.
a tempo
Ab/Db
Gb/Db
Db
death, nor life, nor angels, nor principalities, Nor
75
F7
Div.
3
Bbm add9 Bbm
Ebm7
powers, nor things present, nor things to come,
f

Ebm7/Ab Ab7 ff (79) Db Eb/Db

Not height, nor depth, nor an - y

ff

Ab/C Gb/Bb (83) Ebm7/Ab

crea - ture Shall sep - a - rate me from the love of God,

Ab7 Ebm7 molto rit. Ebm7/Ab Ab7 Gb/Ab

Through Je - sus Christ, our

molto rit. R.H.

(87) Db Eb/Db rit. Db

Lord.

8va 8va

a tempo R.H. rit. 8va ff L.H.

8va 8va 8va

Shut de Dō

R. S.

RANDY STONEHILL
Arr. by Tom Fettke

27
Cued notes optional 4th part
Soprano
Shut de dō, keep out de dev-il. Shut de dō, keep de
Alto
de dō de dev-il. Shut de dō, keep de
31
dev-il in the night.
Shut de dō, keep out de dev-il.
dev-il in the night.
de dō de dev-il.
3rd time to Coda
mp
Light the can - dle, ev-'ry - thin's al - right. Light the can - dle, ev-'ry-
Light the can - dle, ev-'ry - thin's al - right. Light the can - dle, ev-'ry-
1
mf Solo 37
thin's al - right. Oh, Sa-tan is an e - vil charm - er.
thin's al - right.
All
Solo 41
Shut de dō, keep out de dev-il. He's hun-gry for a soul to hurt.
All
45 Solo
Shut de dō, keep de dev-il in the night. And with-out your

All
49 Solo
ho - ly ar - mor— Shut de dō, keep out de dev - il— He will eat you
All
for des - sert! Shut de dō, keep de dev - il in the night.
2
54
thin's al - right. Say der, hey, hey, hey, shut de dō.
thin's al - right. Say der, hey, hey, hey, shut de dō.
58
Hey, hey hey, shut de dō. Hey, hey, you bet - ter
Hey, hey, hey, keep out de dev - il. Hey, hey, hey,
D.S. al Coda
shut de dō. Say a prayer, he won't be back no more.
you bet - ter shut it.
CODA
Optional solo
63
You bet - ter shut de dō. You got - ta
cue notes optional
thin's al - right. Shut de dō, keep out de dev - il.
thin's al - right. de dō, de dev - il.

67
shut de dō,
Whoa,
shut de dō.
Shut de dō, keep de dev - il in the night.
Shut de dō, keep
Shut de dō, keep de dev - il in the night.
de dō,
Chil - dren, light the can - dle, ev - 'ry - thin's al - right.
out de dev - il. Light the can - dle, ev - 'ry - thin's al - right.
de dev - il. Light the can - dle, ev - 'ry - thin's al - right.
71
Whoa,
mp
Light the can - dle, ev - 'ry - thin's al - right.
p
Light the can - dle, ev - 'ry -
75
(ad lib)
rit.
Whoa!
Ev - 'ry - thin's al - right!
sub. ff
thin's al - right. Light the can - dle, ev - 'ry - thin's al - right.

Ten Thousand Angels

R. O.
RAY OVERHOLT
Arr. by Tom Fettke
Expressively, with a slight feeling of rubato ♩ = ca. 84
mf
rit.
1st verse: unison
2nd verse: solo or unison
mp
a tempo
Eb
Db/Eb
Eb7
1. They bound the hands of Je - sus in the
on His pre - cious head they
Ab6/Eb
Abm/Eb
Ab/Eb
Div.
gar - den where He prayed. They led Him through the streets in
placed a crown of thorns; They laughed and said, "Be - hold, the
Unison
Ebsus
Gm7
C9b/7
shame. They spat up-on the Sav - ior, so
king." They struck Him and they cursed Him, and

NOTE: an individual cassette accompaniment tape is available for this arrangement (MU-1205C).

19
Fm7 Bb9 Eb Eb9 Eb7 Ab6 Gm7 Fm7 Ab/Bb Bb7
slight rit.
pure and free from sin. They said, "Cru - ci - fy Him! He's to
mocked His ho - ly name. All a - lone He suf - fered ev - 'ry-
slight rit.
23
Eb Fm7 Eb7/G Ab A°
a tempo and slightly faster
Div.
f
blame." He could have called ten thou - sand
thing.
a tempo and slightly faster
f
27
Eb/Bb Bb7/Ab Eb/G E° Fm7 Bb Bb7 Bb9
an - gels To de - stroy the world and set Him
31
Eb7sus Eb7 Eb9 Ab
ff
free. He could have called ten thou - sand
ff

Eb Bb/D rit. Cm Slowly *mp* Unison Ab AbM7 (35) Gm7 Cm7 Fm7 Bb7

an - gels, But He died a - lone ___ for you and

rit. *mp* Slowly

1 Eb Bb9/Eb *Solo or unison* 2 Eb B7 B9 More freely, a little faster *mf* Unison

me. 2. Up - me. To the

(41) E D/E E7 A/E Am/E E cresc.

howl - ing mob He yield - ed; He did not for mer - cy cry. The

mf cresc.

(45) A/E *Div.* E *Unison* E sus *mp*

cross of shame He took a - lone. ___ And

mp

49
Stricter tempo
E
G♯m7
C♯7 9♭
F♯m7
B9
E
when He cried, "It's fin - ished," He gave him - self to die.
E7
53
A♭
G♯m7 F♯m7
A M7 / B
B7
E
Sal - va - tion's won - drous plan was done.
F♯m7 E7/G♯
57
Div.
f
A
A♯o
E / B
B7 / A
He could have called ten thou - sand an - gels
f
E / G♯
E♯o
61
F♯m7
B
B7
B9
E7sus
E7
To de-stroy the world and set Him free.

E
E7
65
A
rit. ff
ten.
ten.
a tempo
He could have called ten thou - sand
a tempo
E
B/D♯
C♯m
Slowly
G♯m6/B
A
A M7
69
G♯m7
C♯m7
rit.
mp Unison
an - gels, But He died a - lone
Slowly
mp
F♯m7
B7
E
a tempo
for you and me.
a tempo
73
A/E
Am add9/E
E add9
E
(7)
p
ppp
Oo
L.H.
ppp

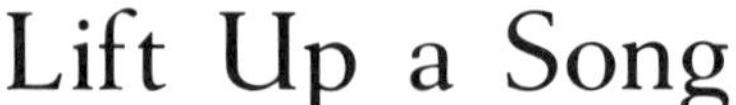

Lift Up a Song

S. F.

STEVE FRY
Arr. by Joseph Linn
SSA arr. by Tom Fettke

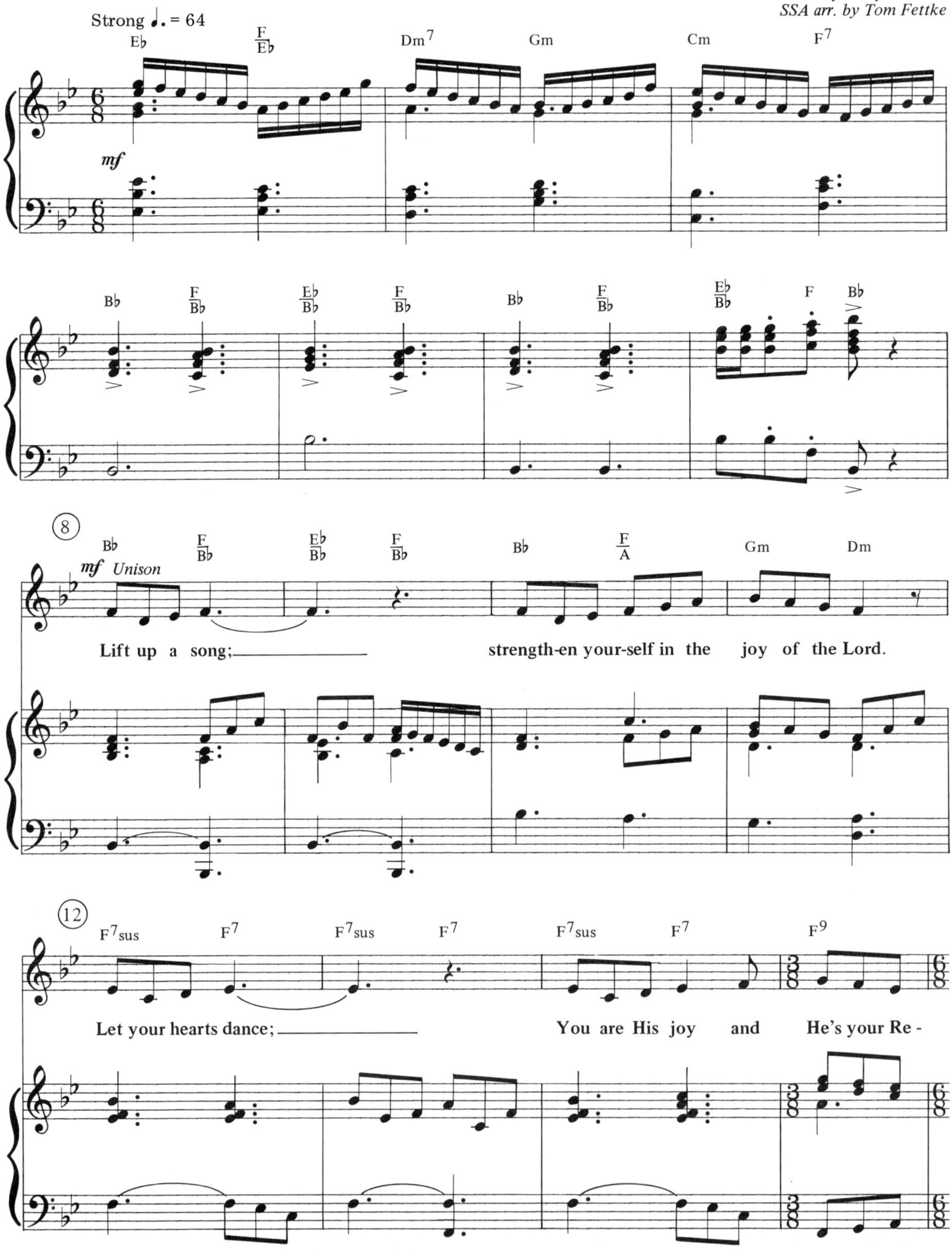

Strong ♩. = 64
E♭ F/E♭ Dm7 Gm Cm F7
mf
B♭ F/B♭ E♭/B♭ F/B♭ B♭ F/B♭ E♭/B♭ F B♭
8
B♭ F/B♭ E♭/B♭ F/B♭ B♭ F/A Gm Dm
mf Unison
Lift up a song; strength-en your-self in the joy of the Lord.
12
F7sus F7 F7sus F7 F7sus F7 F9
Let your hearts dance; You are His joy and He's your Re -

NOTE: an individual cassette accompaniment tape is available for this arrangement (MU-1202C).

18
Bb
F/Bb
1st and 2nd Sop.
Div.
Lift up your hands;
Alto
ward.
Lift up your hands;
To-
Unison
Gm
Dm
Cm
F7
geth-er we are the new tem-ple that fol-lows His lov-ing com-mands.
24
Eb
Div.
N.C.
We are the tem-ple, the bod-y, the bride of the Lamb.
He is a-
28
Bbsus Bb
mong us
danc-ing and sing-ing,
Unison
Sing-ing with

32
joy o-ver all the re - deemed who are com-ing to Zi - on. Be - hold, His
36
pres-ence comes to His tem-ple, As the re -
Div.
40
deemed of the Lord join the dance of the Pass - o - ver Lamb.
44

48
1st and 2nd Sop.
Lift up a song;
Alto
Lift up a song;
Unison
strength-en your-self in the joy of the Lord.
52
Div.
Let your heart dance;
Let your heart dance;
Unison
you are His joy and He's your Re-
ward.
58
Div.
Lift up your hands;
Lift up your hands; to-
Unison
geth-er we are the new tem-ple that fol-lows His lov-ing com-mands.

64
Dm Em F G C F/C G C N.C.
Div.
We are the tem-ple, the bod-y, the bride of the Lamb. Oh, it is
68
C/F F Csus C
Je - sus, the Lamb who has saved us, Who now has been
72
G F G Gsus Csus C G/C F/C
raised and is seat - ed in pow'r at the hand of the Fa - ther.
C
76
C/F F G/F G/F F Csus C
Be-hold His pres-ence comes to His tem-ple,

80
G
Unison
F
G
G7
C
F/C
G/C
As the re - deemed of the Lord join the dance of the Pass - o - ver Lamb,
C
Div.
84
G
Unison
F
G
G7
C
F/C
G/C
As the re - deemed of the Lord join the dance of the Pass - o - ver Lamb,
C
Div.
88
G
F
G
As the re - deemed of the Lord join the dance of the Pass - o - ver
C
G/C
91
F/C
G sus
C
G/C
F/C
C
Lamb, the Pass - o - ver Lamb.

We've Come, O Lord

D. N.

DON NEUFELD
SSA arr. by Tom Fettke

28
rit.
slightly slower
1st Sop.
mp
gain the strength to live for You In days that lie a - head, In days to
33
mp
come. We've come to seek Your face, O Lord; We've
mp
37
come to wor-ship You. We've come to set our - selves a - part For
42
rit.
mf
A - men, a - men,
You this qui - et hour. A - men,
mf
A - men, a - men,
a - men.
decresc.
a - men, a - men, a - men.
decresc.
a - men, a - men.

I Will Glory in the Cross

D. R.

DOTTIE RAMBO
Arr. by Joseph Linn
SSA arr. by Tom Fettke

NOTE: an individual cassette accompaniment tape is available for this arrangement (MU-1223C).

18
22
30
34
mf
mp
Div.
All glo - ry and praise shall rest up - on
Him, So will - ing to die in my place.
I will glo - ry in the cross, in the cross, Lest His
suf - f'ring all be in vain.
I will weep no

B♭m7/E♭ E♭7 A♭ 2nd time to Coda A♭m/F A♭m6 38 E♭/B♭ B♭6 B♭7
more for the cross that He bore; I will glo - ry in the
E♭ D♭/E♭ E♭ D♭/E♭ Unison mf
cross. My
44 March-like A♭ C♭/A♭ D♭/A♭ C/A♭ 48 A♭ Div. D♭/A♭
tro - phies and crowns, my robe stained with sin Was all that I
A♭ B♭/A♭ D♭/E♭ E♭ D♭/E♭ E♭ Fm7 E♭7/G 53 A♭
had to lay at His feet; Un - wor - thy to
feet, His feet;

Gb/Ab Ab7 Db Dbm6 57 Ab/Eb Eb Db/Eb Eb7
Unison
eat from the ta - ble of life 'Til love made pro - vi - sion for
Ab AbGm Fm7 Ab/Bb
D.S. al Coda
CODA
Abm/F Abm6 62 Eb/Bb
Build to the end
me. I will bore; I will glo - ry, I will
Build to the end
F/Bb 66 Gb/Eb F/Eb
glo - ry, glo - ry, glo - ry
E M7/Eb 70 Eb
in, in the cross.
8va

How Majestic Is Your Name

M. W. S.
Based on Psalm 8:1, Isaiah 9:6

MICHAEL W. SMITH
Arr. by Joseph Linn
SSA arr. by Tom Fettke

Energetically
F C/E F C/E Dm7 C/E F G Am7 G7/B
C G C G
5
F C/E F C/E Dm7 C/E Dm7 G Am7 G7/B
C
Unison
mf
9
Oh Lord, our Lord, how ma - jes - tic is Your name in all the
mf
G G/B C
13
earth. Oh, Lord, our Lord, how ma - jes - tic is Your name in all the

NOTE: an individual cassette accompaniment tape is available for this arrangement (MU-2031C).

17
G G/B C F C/E F C/E Dm7 Dm7 C/E F G Am7
f
earth. Oh, Lord, we praise
cresc.
f
G7/B C G C F C/E F C/E Dm7 C/E F
mf
f
Your name. Oh, Lord, we
mf
cresc.
21
G Am7 G7/B C B B7/D♯ Em D D7/F♯
25
mag - ni - fy Your name: Prince of Peace, might - y
f
G G/F C/E F G sus G7
Unison
God; Oh, Lord God Al - might -

29
C G C G C G C
y.
31
D A D A D A D
Alto
mf
Oh,
mf
33
1st and 2nd sop.
D
Unison
D/F♯
cresc.
G A/G G A/G
Div.
cued notes opt.
D D/F♯
f
Oh, Lord, how ma - jes - tic is Your name on
Alto
cresc.
f
Lord, our Lord, how ma - jes - tic is Your name in all the
cresc.
f
A A/C♯ D
37
Unison
mf
D/F♯
cresc.
G A/G G A/G
Div.
earth. Oh, Lord, how ma - jes - tic is Your
mf
cresc.
earth. Oh, Lord, our Lord, how ma - jes - tic is Your
mf
cresc.

41
name on earth. Oh, Lord,
name in all the earth. Oh, Lord,
we praise Your name. Oh, Lord,
45
we magnify Your name: Prince of Peace, mighty
49
cresc.
mf
f

A A/G D/F♯ G Em7/A A 1 D A D
mf
God; Oh, Lord God Al - might - y. Oh,
mf
2 D A/D D Em7/D A/D D
56
p
y. Lord, how ma- jes - tic (ih)
(A cappella preferred)
pp
is Your name. Lord, how ma-jes - tic (ih) is Your name. Oh,
mp
mf
p
60
cresc.
G D/F♯ G D/F♯ Em7 Em7 D/F♯ G A Bm7 A/C♯
f
Lord, we praise Your
mf cresc.

D A D
64
G D/F♯ G D/F♯ Em7 Em7 D/F♯ G
Sop. 1
Oh, Lord,
cresc.
mf
name. Lord, how ma-jes - tic (ih) is Your name; We
mp
cresc.
A Bm7 A7/C♯ D C♯ C♯9/E♯
68
F♯m C♯m F♯m C♯m F♯m
mag - ni - fy Your name Prince of Peace,
mf
E A E A E A A A/G
72
D/F♯
f
might - y God. Oh, Lord
G Em7/A A7 D A/D D G A D
God Al - might - y, how ma-jes - tic (ih) is Your name.

God Exalted Him

LINDA LEE JOHNSON
Based on Philippians 2:5-11

TOM FETTKE

Note: an individual cassette accompaniment tape is available for this arrangement (MU-2085C).

17
Div. optional
To be a car - pen-ter, a sim - ple car - pen-ter,
Still He be - came a man— a gen - tle, lov - ing man,
21
Unison
slight accel.
A low - ly ser - vant, re - ject - ed by His own.
A man of sor - row, ac - quaint - ed with grief.
slight accel.
1st Sop., 2nd Sop., 1st Alto
♩ = ca. 100
f
25
Div.
But God ex - alt - ed Him, God has up -
Optional 2nd Alto
f
25
f

29
lift - ed Him,
And has giv - en Him a
29
name a - bove all names;
33
That ev - 'ry knee should bow
33
in earth and heav'n a - bove,
And ev - 'ry

37
slight rit. and decresc.
Beginning
1
freely
D.S.
tongue con - fess that Je - sus Christ is Lord.
37
1
D.S
slight rit. and decresc.
freely
2
a tempo
Stronger
43
Lord. God has ex - alt - ed Him,
2
Stronger
43
a tempo
God has up - lift - ed Him, And has

giv - en Him a name a - bove all names;
51
That ev - 'ry knee should bow in earth and
51
heav'n a - bove, And ev - 'ry tongue con - fess that
55
55

Jesus Christ is Lord.
ff
60
rit. and dim.
And ev'ry tongue confess that Jesus Christ is
63
mf
(6)
Lord; He is Lord, He is Lord.

Lord, Let Me Serve—Medley

Arr. by Doug Holck
SSA arr. by Tom Fettke

Rubato
mp
In tempo ♩ = ca. 96
7
*"Lord, Let Me Serve" (Linda Lee Johnson - Tom Fettke)
With feeling
mp Unison
Lord, let me serve;
Lord, let me fol - low.
11
Give me a place and a
pur - pose to fill.
Teach me to serve,

(19)

teach me to fol - low; Use me to do ___ Your

(23)

rit.

will. ___

rit.

*"This Is My Prayer" (Doug Holck)

Div.

I want to love You, Lord;

(27)

I want to serve You, Lord;

Unison 3

I want to please You, Lord;

This is my pray'r.

(31)

mf *Div.*

I want to love You, Lord;

mf

35
Unison
I want to serve You, Lord; I want to please You, Lord;
This is my pray'r.
39
mf Div.
f
I want to love You, Lord;
mf
f
I want to serve You, Lord;
44
3
I want to please You, Lord;
This is my pray'r.
f
I want to
f

(48)

love You, Lord; I want to serve You, Lord; I want to

(52)

please You, Lord; This is my pray'r.

(56)

1st and 2nd Sop. *mp* I want to serve You, Lord;

Alto *mp* Lord, let me serve; Lord, let me

l.h. *mp*

fol - low;

(61) Slowing

1st Sop. This is my pray'r. *p*

2nd Sop. and Alto This is my pray'r, my pray'r.

Slowing *p*

I'm Climbing up the Mountain

M. L.

MOSIE LISTER
Arr. by Joseph Linn
SSA arr. by Tom Fettke

NOTE: an individual cassette accompaniment tape is available for this arrangement (MU-2062C).

F
Gm/F
F
F
A7/C♯
Dm
17
F
D7
G7
Div.
more, no more; And I'll reach the oth-er side
C7
F
B♭/F
F
F7
21
B♭
E♭/B♭
B♭
by and by, by and by. Well, well, I'm climb-in' up the
E♭/B♭
B♭
F
moun-tain to the sky. I'm
25
B♭/F
F
B♭/F
F
C7
go-ing where I'll nev-er, nev-er die, nev-er

Dm/C C^6 C^7 (29) F

die. I'm climb-in' up the moun-tain, climb-in'

(33) F D^7

high-er up the moun-tain; And I'll reach the oth-er

G^7 C^7 F *Unison* D^7

side by and by. Well, I

(37) G D^7 G Am/G G

would not keep a - sin-nin', oh no, oh

Div.
no; I'm trav-'ling with my Je-sus to the sky.
1st and 2nd Sop.: And I start-ed, start-ed trav-'ling long a-
I start-ed, start-ed trav-'ling long a-
go, go, long a - go; And I'll reach the oth - er
side by and by, by and by. Well, well, I'm

53
C
F/C C
F/C C
G
climb-in' up the moun-tain to the sky.
57
C/G G
C/G G
D7
I'm go-ing where I'll nev-er, nev-er die, nev-er
D7
Em/D
D6
D7
61
G
die. I'm climb-in' up the moun-tain, climb-in'
65
G
E7
high-er up the moun-tain; And I'll reach the oth-er

68
A7
D7
G/F
C/E
side by and by. I'm climb-in' up the
G/D
C
G/B
A7/C♯
moun-tain, climb-in' high-er up the moun-tain; And I'll
72
G/D
E7
A7
D7
G
C/G
reach the oth-er side by and by, by and
G
Am/G
76
G
C/G
G
cued 4th part opt.
by, by and by, by and by!

The Love of God
F. M. L.
F. M. LEHMAN
Arr. by Doug Holck
SSA arr. by Tom Fettke
Rubato, slow and with feeling
r.h.
l.h.
mp
6
In tempo ♩ = ca. 72
Unison mp
The love of God is great-er
In tempo
10
far Than tongue or pen can ev-er tell; It goes be-yond the high-est
14
mf
Div.
star And reach-es to the low-est hell. The guilt-y pair bowed down with
mf

18
care God gave His Son to win; His err - ing child He rec - on-
ciled And par-doned from his sin. O love of
3
23
f
mf
God, how rich and pure; How mea-sure - less and
f
mf
27
f
mf
strong! It shall for - ev - er-more en - dure The saints' and
f
mf

31
mp
an - gels' song.
mp
Solo or unison
mp
Could we with
35
With feeling
ink the o - cean fill
And were the skies of parch-ment
39
made, Were ev - 'ry stalk on earth a quill
And ev-'ry

43
1st Sop.: To write the love of God a-
All mf
man a scribe by trade,
2nd Sop. and Alto: To write the love
mf
bove Would drain the o - cean dry, Nor could the
mf
of God a-bove Would drain the o - cean dry, Nor could the
mf
47
scroll con-tain the whole
scroll, could the scroll con-tain the whole Though stretched from sky to
3
molto rit.
ten.
52
a tempo
sky. O love of God, how rich and
ten.
a tempo
molto rit.
f

pure; How mea-sure - less and strong! It shall for-
56
ev - er-more en - dure The saints' and an - gels'
slight accel.
60
song. Oh, love, the love of
slight accel.
8va
God, the love of God.
ff
ff
3
3
rit.
8va
8va

His Grace Is Sufficient for Me

M. L.

MOSIE LISTER
SSA arr. by Tom Fettke

Expressively ♩ = 100
Eb 9/6
Gb 13/11♯/9
Fm9
E 11♯/9
mf
Flowing
5
Eb 9/6
Gb9
Fm11
Ab/Bb
1st verse: Unison melody (alto part)
2nd verse: 2 parts (2nd sop. and alto on melody)
mel.
1. Man - y
(2. When the)
Eb
Bb7
Gm
Gbo
times I'm tried and test-ed as I trav - el day by day. Oft I
tempt-er brings con - fu-sion and I don't know what to do, On my
13
Fm
Bb7
Eb
Ab
Eb
meet with pain and sor-row and there's trou-ble in the way; But I
knees I turn to Je - sus for I know He'll see me through. Then de-

17
G G7 Cm Ab
have the sweet as - sur-ance that my soul the Lord will lead, And in
spair is changed to vic-t'ry, ev - 'ry doubt just melts a - way, And in
21
Eb/Bb C7 F7 Bb7 2nd time to Coda Eb Ab Eb Gm Gbo
Him there is strength for ev - 'ry need. Oh, His
Him there is hope for ev - 'ry
25
Fm Bb7 Eb Ab Eb Gm Gbo
grace is suf - fi - cient for me, And His
29
Fm Bb7 Eb Ab Eb Div.
love is a - bun-dant and free; And what

(33) E♭ A♭ G Cm A♭

joy fills my soul just to know, just to know That His

(37) E♭/B♭ C7 F7 B♭7 E♭ *D.S. al Coda* B♭7

1st Sop.

2nd Sop. and Alto

grace is suf - fi - cient for me. When the

CODA E♭ (42) B7 *Unison* G°/B F♯m B7

day. Oh, His grace is suf - fi - cient for

E C7 A♭°/C (47) Gm C7

me, And His love is a - bun-dant and

F
Div.
51
B♭
free; And what joy fills my soul just to
A Dm B♭ 55 F/C D7 G7 C7
know, just to know That His grace is suf - fi-cient for
1 F 2 F 60 B♭
me. And what me. Oh, His
F/C no decresc. D7 G7 C7 F (6+)
grace is suf - fi-cient for me.
no decresc.

Ceaseless Praise

FRANCES R. HAVERGAL

TOM FETTKE

love.
2
2
on - ly, for my King.
2
mf
16
f
Lord, I give my life to Thee; Thine for-ev-er-more to be.
f
20
Div.
rit.
2nd time to Coda
Lord, I give my life to Thee; Thine for - ev - er - more to
rit.
25
be.
Freely
mp
accel.

(29) a tempo
Flowing ♩ = ca. 76

mp 1. Take my sil - ver and my gold; Not a mite would I with-
mf 2. Take my will and make it Thine; It shall be no lon - ger

mp-mf

(33)

hold. Take my mo-ments and my days; Let them flow in cease-less
mine. Take my heart; it is Thine own; It shall

1

praise.

mf

2

D.S. al Coda

be Thy roy - al throne.

CODA

Very intense

p

rit.

be, Thine for - ev - er - more to be.

p

rit.

Christlike Medley

Including
He's Still Workin' on Me
Let the Beauty of Jesus Be Seen in Me
2 Corinthians 3:18

Arr. by Tom Fettke

*Cued note 1st Sop. 2nd verse only.

"Let the Beauty of Jesus Be Seen in Me"
(A. W. T. Orsborn - T. Jones)
D.S. twice
CODA
24
28
32
Unison
Div.
F
B♭/F
C7
D♭
D♭/F
A♭7/E♭
A♭7
E♭m7
A♭9
E°
hand.
clay.
me!
Let the beau-ty of Je-sus be seen in me—
All His won-der-ful pas-sion and pu-ri-ty!
O Thou Spir-it di-vine, All my

36
G♭/D♭
D♭
D♭°
A♭7/E♭
D♭/F
G♭
B♭m6
na - ture re - fine,
Till
the
beau - ty of Je - sus be
D♭/A♭
A♭7
40
Cm7
F7
seen
in
me.
44
E♭/F
B♭
B♭+
E♭
F7/E♭
"2 Corinthians 3:18" (Unknown)
From
glo - ry to glo - ry He's
48
Unison
chang - ing me,
Chang - ing me,

52
Div.
Bb
Bb+
Eb
F7/Eb
Eb
changing me; His likeness and image per-
56
Bb
Eb/Bb
Bb
Eb
Cm7
F7
Eb/F
F7
fecting in me The love of God shown to the
60
Bb
F7/C
Bb/D
F
F7
world. For He's changing,
64
Bb
F7/Bb
Bb
Bb/D
F7
Eb/Bb
F7
changing me From earthly things into

68
B♭
F/B♭
E♭
F7/E♭
B♭+
heav - en - ly; His like - ness and im - age per -
72
E♭/B♭
B♭/D
Cm
F7
E♭/F
fect - ing in me the love of God shown to the
1
F
2
world. From world. The
78
Cm7
F9sus
love of God shown to the world.
(6)

Jesus, the Very Thought of Thee

A Meditation

Including
Sun of My Soul
Jesus, the Very Thought of Thee
Fairest Lord Jesus

Arr. by Tom Fettke

With warmth

mp "Sun of My Soul" (Katholisches Gesangbuch - John Keble)

p *Optional 2nd alto part*

Sun of my soul, Thou Sav - ior dear,

5 It is not night if Thou be near.

9 O may no earth - born clouds a - rise

13 rit. To hide Thee from Thy ser - vant's eyes.

17
"Jesus, the Very Thought of Thee" (Bernard of Clairvaux, tr. Caswall - Dykes)
a tempo
mf
1. Je - sus, the ver - y thought of Thee
2. O Hope of ev - 'ry con - trite heart,
1st sop. With sweet - ness fills my breast;
1st alto O Joy of all the meek,
2nd sop. With sweet - ness fills my (pp) Je - sus, Je - sus;
2nd alto O Joy of all the (pp) Je - sus, Je - sus;
25
But sweet - er far Thy face to see,
To those who fail, how kind Thou art!
29
rit.
1 Repeat optional
2
And in Thy pres - ence rest.
How good to those who seek!
33
a tempo
mf "Fairest Lord Jesus" (Gesangbuch, tr. Seiss - H. A. Hoffman)
Fair - est Lord Je - sus! Rul - er of all

37
na - ture! O Thou of God and
41
man the Son! Thee will I cher - ish,
45
Thee will I hon - or, Thou, my soul's glo - ry,
48
Slower
gradual decresc.
joy, and crown! Sun of my soul, Thou
rit.
p
Sav - ior dear. A - men.

Heaven's Jubilee
ADGER M. PACE
G. T. SPEER
Arr. by Mosie Lister
SSA arr. by Tom Fettke
Driving
G D/F♯ Em A7 G/D D6 D7 G C/G G
mf
6
G Am7 G/B C G/D D7 G
mf Unison
Some glad morn - ing we shall see___ Je - sus in the air,
When with all that heav'n-ly host___ we be - gin to sing,
mf
10
Em B Em A7 D
Com - ing af - ter you and me–___ joy is ours to share.
Sing - ing in the Ho - ly Ghost,___ how the heav'ns will ring.
14
G Am7 Bm C G/D D7 G
What re - joic - ing there will be___ when the saints shall rise,
Mil - lions there will join the song,___ with them we shall be

18
Div.
D/F♯ Em A7 G/D D7sus D7 G
Head - ed for the ju - bi - lee yon - der in the skies.
Prais - ing Christ thro' a - ges long; what a ju - bi - lee!
23
G Em G D
Oh, what sing - ing; Oh, what
What a day of sing - ing, sing - ing; What a day of
G
shout - ing
27
D/A G/B Em A7
shout - ing, shout - ing On that hap - py morn - ing when we all shall
D
rise.
31
G Em G D
Oh, what glo - ry, Hal - le -
What a day of glo - ry, glo - ry, Glo - ry hal - le -

G
lu - jah
35
D/F♯
Em
A7
G/D
D7
lu - jah, glo - ry When we meet our bless - ed Sav - ior in the
G
1
D.C.
2
E♭7
skies.
8va
8va loco
43
A♭
Fm
A♭
E♭
Oh, what sing - ing, Oh, what
What a day of sing - ing, sing - ing, What a day of
f
A♭
shout - ing
47
E♭/B♭
A♭/C
Fm
B♭7
shout - ing, shout - ing On that hap - py morn - ing when we all shall

Eb — (51) Ab — Fm — Ab — Eb

Oh what glo - ry, Hal - le -

rise. What a day of glo - ry, glo - ry, Glo - ry, hal - le -

Ab — (55) Eb/G — Fm — Bb7 — Ab/Eb — Eb7

lu - jah

lu - jah, glo - ry When we meet our bless - ed Sav - ior in the

Ab — (59) Eb/G — Fm — Bb — Ab/Eb

skies. When we meet our bless - ed Sav - ior in

Eb — (63) Ab

the skies.

Near the Cross

FANNY J. CROSBY

WILLIAM H. DOANE
Arr. by Dick Bolks
SSA arr. by Tom Fettke

21
mf
tain.
In the Cross, in the Cross
mf
25
Be my glo - ry ev - er,
29
1st and 2nd Sop. Till my
rap - tured
Till my soul shall find
33
Rest be - yond the
mp
37
riv - er.

41
mf Unison
Near the Cross! O Lamb of God,
mf
45
49
Bring its scenes be - fore me; Help me
53
walk from day to day With its shad - ows
57
mf
Div.
o'er me. In the Cross, in the
mf

61
Cross Be my glo - ry ev - er,
65
Unison
Till my rap - tured soul shall find Rest be -
69
yond the riv - er.
73
81
f With strength
Near the Cross I'll watch and
With strength
f

85
wait, Hop - ing, trust - ing ev - er,
89
Div.
Till I reach the gold - en strand,
93
Just be - yond the riv - er.
97
mf
In the Cross, in the Cross
101
Be my
mf Optional 4th part
In the Cross, in the Cross Be my
mf

105
glo - ry ev - er, Till my rap - tured
glo - ry ev - er, Till my rap - tured
110
Unison
mf
soul shall find Rest be - yond the riv -
soul shall find Rest
f
mf
gradual dim.
rit.
er.
gradual dim.
rit.
mp

The Birthday of a King

W. H. N.

W. H. NEIDLINGER
Arr. by Tom Fettke

Freely and smoothly
mp
cresc.
5
In tempo ♩ = 80
mf
In the lit - tle vil-lage of Beth - le-hem There lay a
In tempo
mf
Child one day;
10
And the sky was bright with a ho - ly light O'er the
place where Je - sus lay.
14
Al - le - lu - ia! Oh, how the

an - gels sang! Al - le - lu - ia! How it rang! And the
18
sky was bright with a ho - ly light; 'Twas the
Unison
2nd time to Coda
22
birth - day of a king. Let us a - dore Him; O
Div.
come, let us a - dore Him; O come, let us a - dore Him,

29
Solo or unison
Christ, the Lord. 'Twas a hum - ble birth-place but, oh, how much God
33
gave to us that day! From the man - ger bed, what a path has led! What a
D.S. al Coda
All f
CODA
per - fect, ho - ly way! Al - le - King. Al - le -
38
L'istesso Maestoso
Div.
lu - ia! Oh, how the an - gels sang! Al - le - lu - ia!

42
How it rang! And the sky was bright with a
ho - ly light; 'Twas the birth - day of a Sav - ior. Al - le -
cresc. poco a poco
cresc. poco a poco
46
lu - ia! Al - le - lu - ia! 'Twas the birth - day
49
ff
of a king!
ff